4   **Any Dream Will Do**

11   **Happy Birthday to You**

8   **Heart and Soul**

12   **Hi-Lili, Hi-Lo**

16   **If I Only Had a Brain**

20   **Peter Cottontail**

24   **Sing**

28   **The Syncopated Clock**

34   **We're Off to See the Wizard**

31   **When I Grow Too Old to Dream**

Any Dream Will Do

from JOSEPH AND THE AMAZING TECHNICOLOR® DREAMCOAT

Music by Andrew Lloyd Webber
Lyrics by Tim Rice

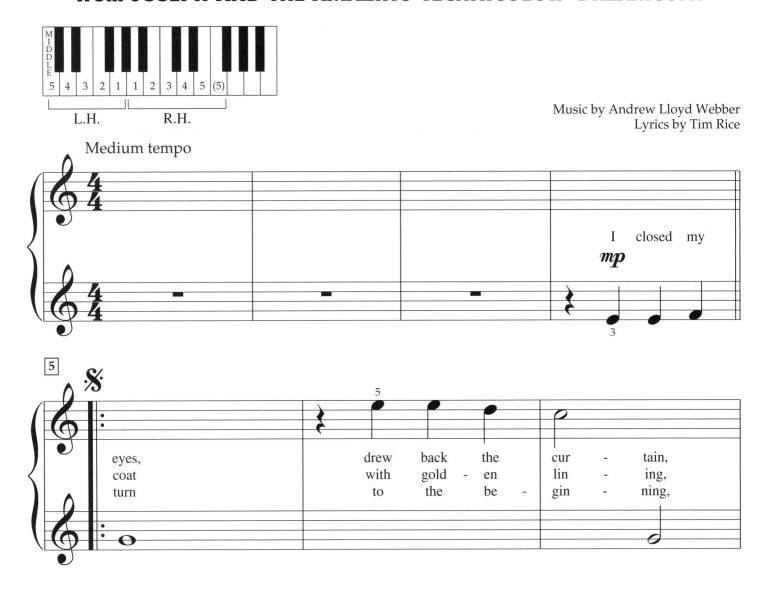

Duet Part (Student plays one octave higher than written.)

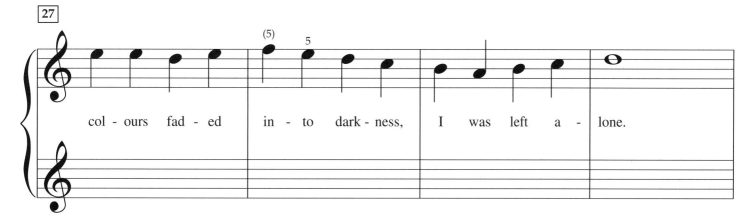

col - ours fad - ed | in - to dark - ness, | I was left a - | lone.

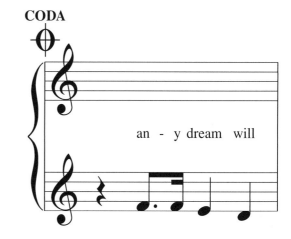

D.S. al Coda

May I re - | an - y dream will

mp

do, | an - y dream will | do. _____

rit.

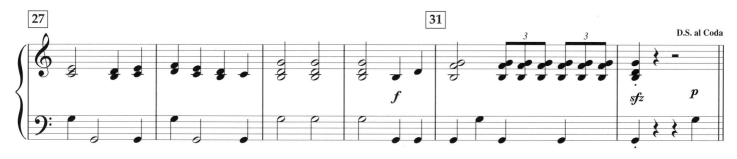

D.S. al Coda

f

sfz   *p*

CODA

rit.

p

Heart and Soul
from the Paramount Short Subject A SONG IS BORN

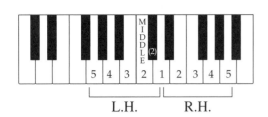

Words by Frank Loesser
Music by Hoagy Carmichael

With a lilt

Heart and soul _____ I fell in love with you. Heart and soul _____
Heart and soul _____ I begged to be a - dored. Lost con - trol _____

_____ the way a fool would do, mad - ly, be - cause you held me
_____ and tum - bled o - ver - board, glad - ly, that mag - ic night we

Duet Part (Student plays one octave higher than written.)

With a lilt

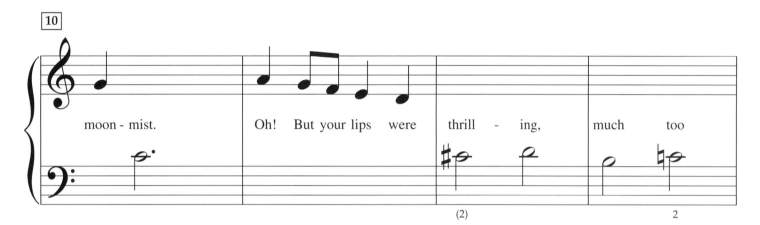

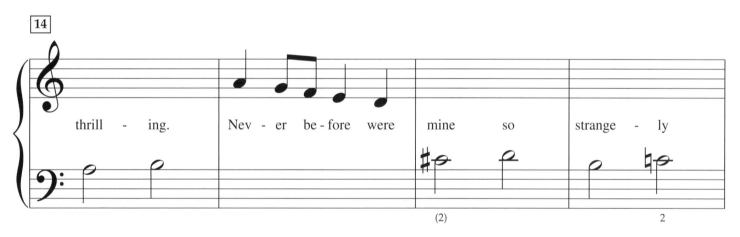

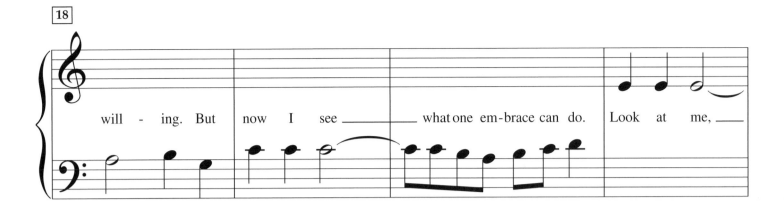

Happy Birthday to You

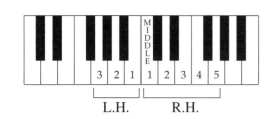

Words and Music by Mildred J. Hill
and Patty S. Hill

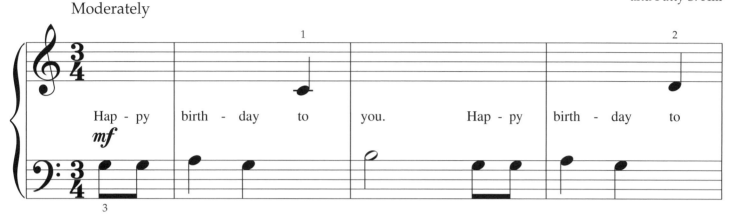

Duet Part (Student plays one octave higher than written.)

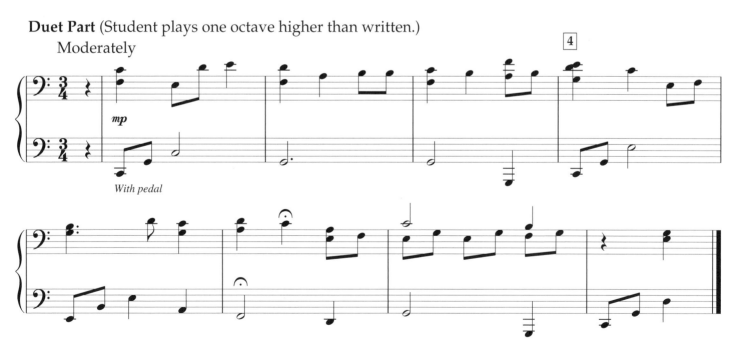

Hi-Lili, Hi-Lo

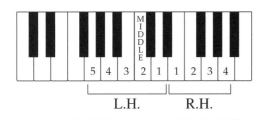

Words by Helen Deutsch
Music by Bronislau Kaper

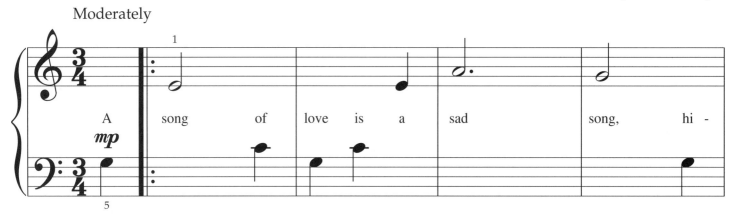

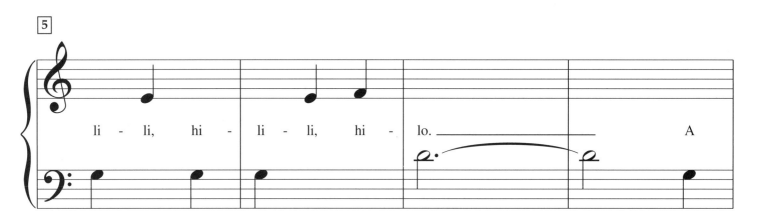

Duet Part (Student plays one octave higher than written.)

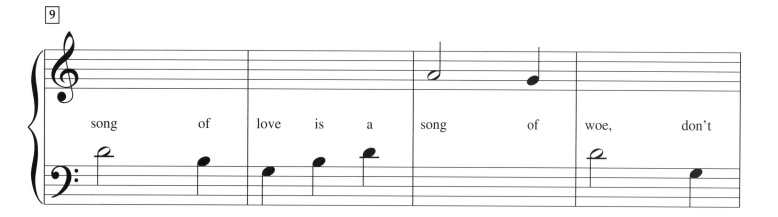

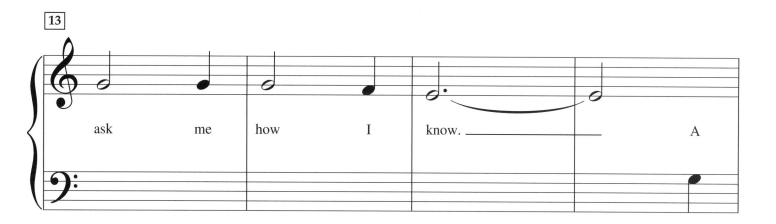

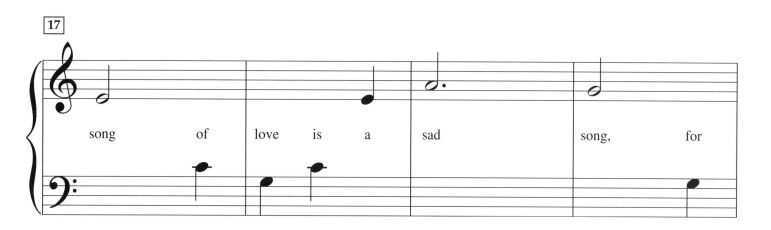

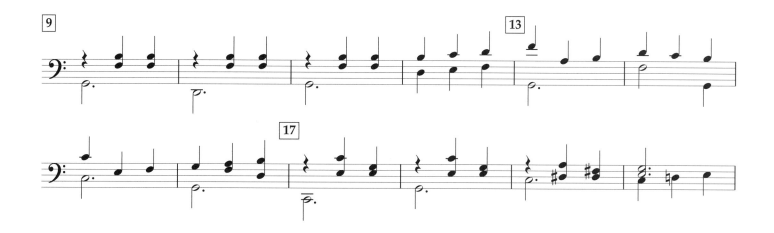

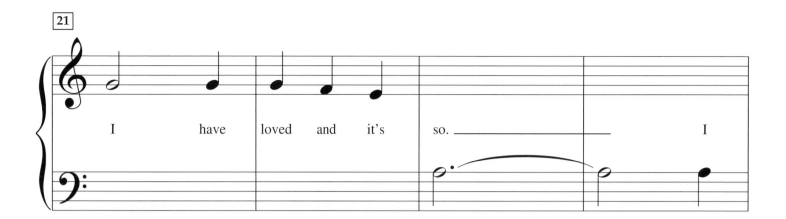
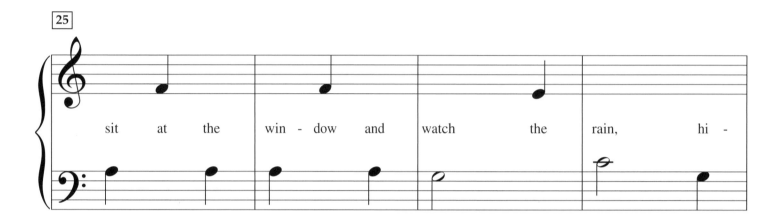
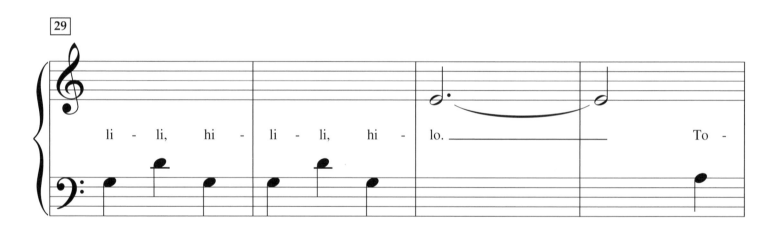

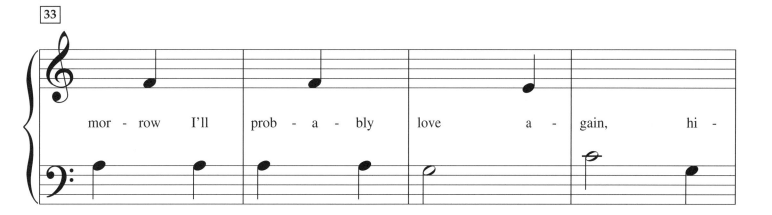

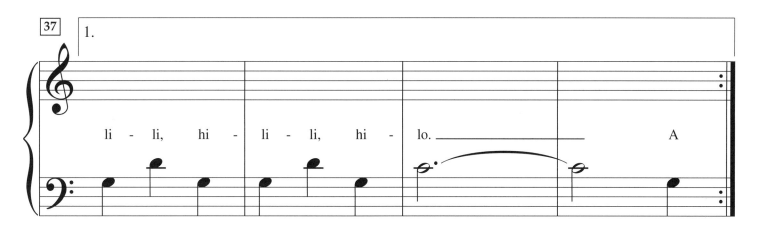

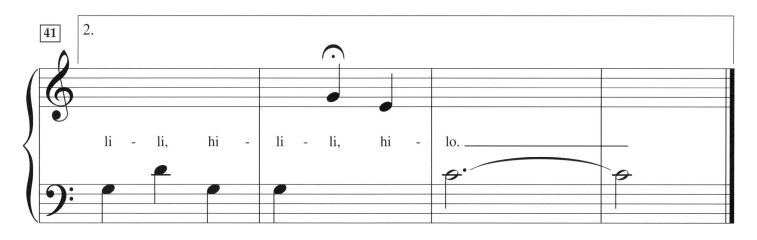

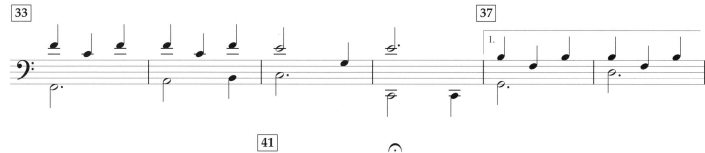

If I Only Had a Brain

from THE WIZARD OF OZ

Lyric by E.Y. "Yip" Harburg
Music by Harold Arlen

Duet Part (Student plays one octave higher than written.)

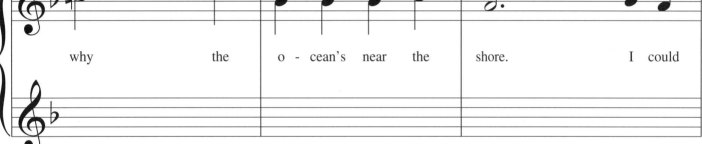

Additional lyrics

2. When a man's an empty kettle, he should be on his mettle and yet, I'm torn apart.
   Just because I'm presumin' that I could be kinda human if I only had a heart.
   I'd be tender, I'd be gentle and awful sentimental regarding love and art.
   I'd be friends with the sparrows and the boy that shoots the arrows, if I only had a heart.
   Picture me a balcony. Above a voice sings low, "Wherefore art thou, Romeo?"
   I hear a beat. How sweet!
   Just to register emotion, jealousy, devotion, and really feel the part,
   I would stay young and chipper and I'd lock it with a zipper, if I only had a heart.

3. Life is sad, believe me, missy, when you're born to be a sissy, without the vim and verve.
   But I could change my habits, nevermore be scared of rabbits if I only had the nerve.
   I'm afraid there's no denyin' I'm just a dandylion, a fate I don't deserve.
   But I could show my prowess, be a lion, not a mowess, if I only had the nerve.
   Oh, I'd be in my stride, a king down to the core. Oh, I'd roar the way I never roared before,
   and then I'd rrrrwoof, and roar some more.
   I would show the dinosaurus, who's king around the forres', a king they better serve.
   Why, with my regal beezer, I could be another Caesar, if I only had the nerve.

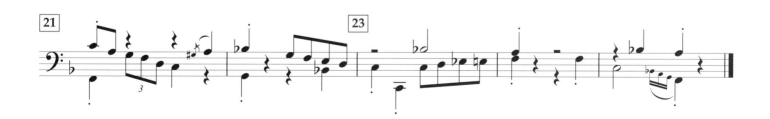

Peter Cottontail

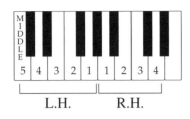

Words and Music by Steve Nelson
and Jack Rollins

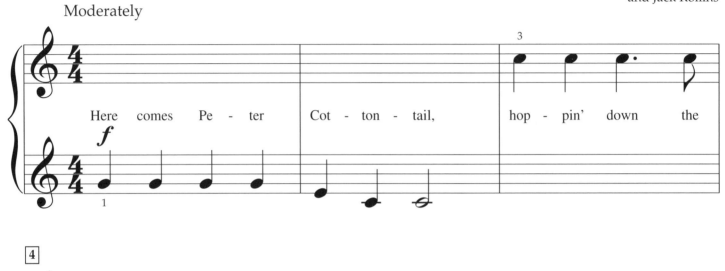

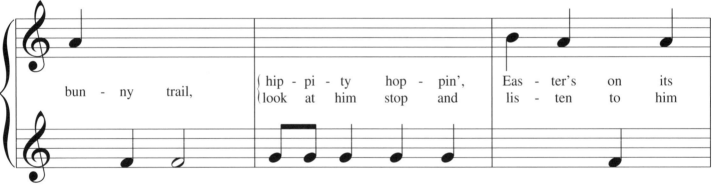

Duet Part (Student plays one octave higher than written.)

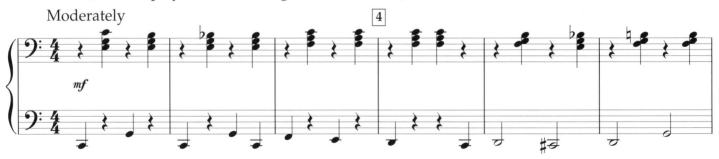

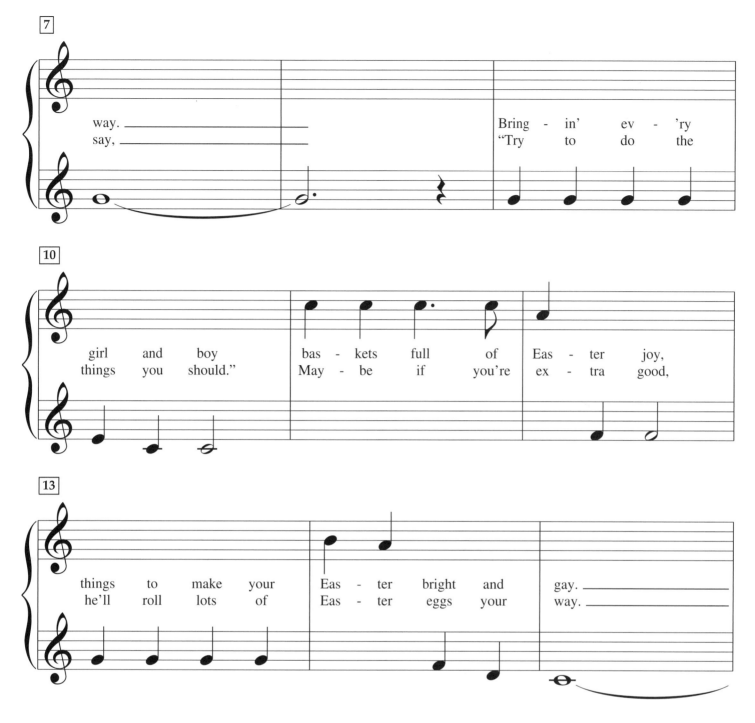

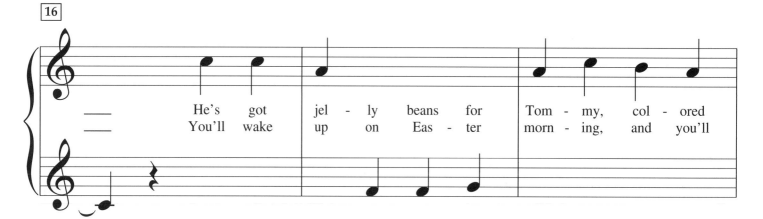

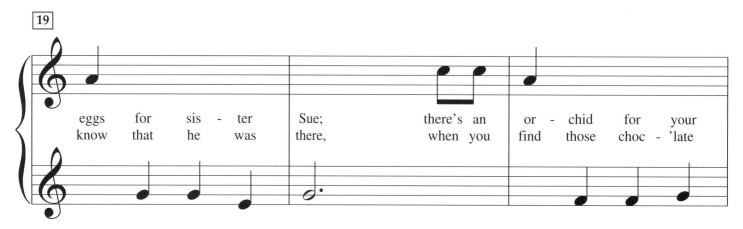

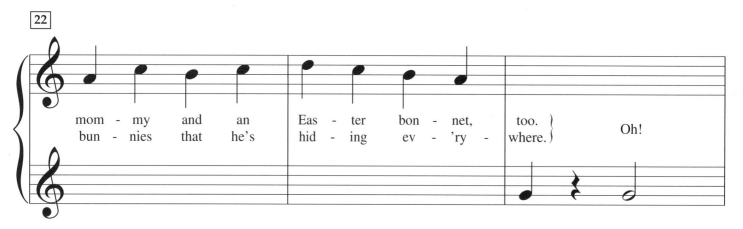

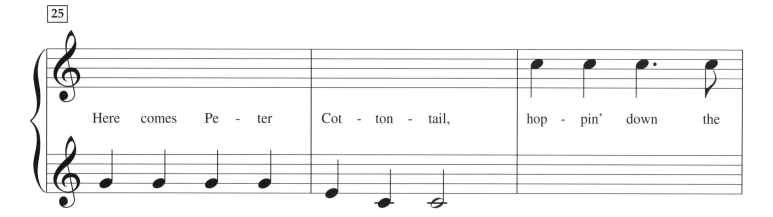

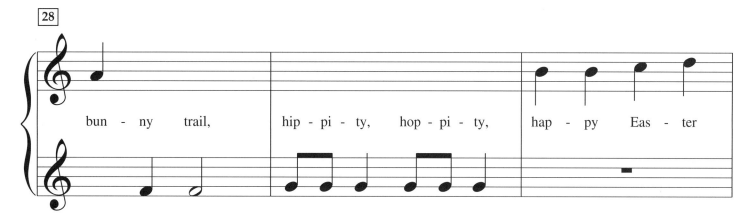

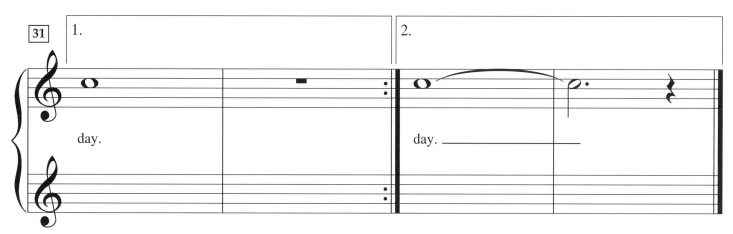

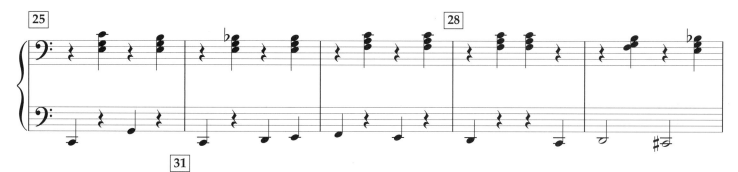

Sing
from SESAME STREET

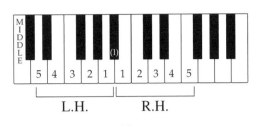

Words and Music by
Joe Raposo

Sing! _____ Sing a

Duet Part (Student plays one octave higher than written.)

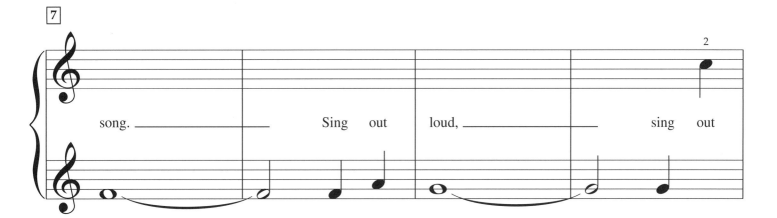

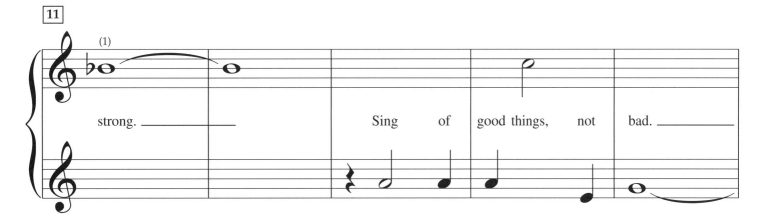

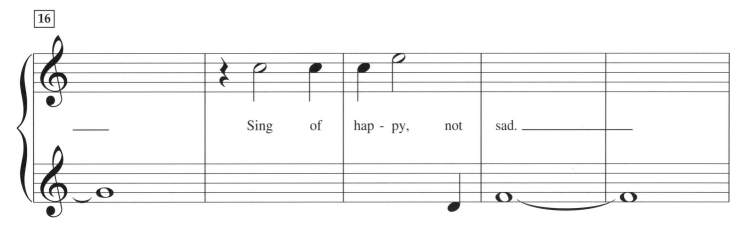

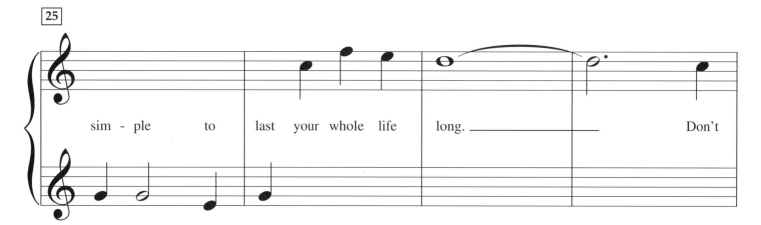

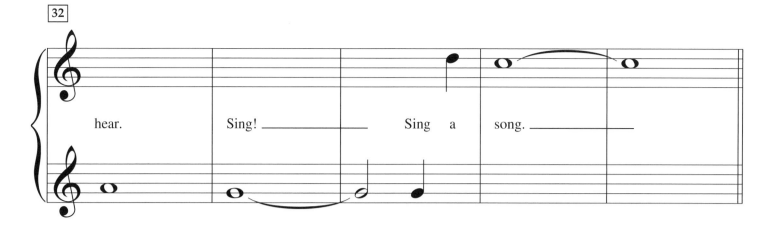

hear.   Sing! _____   Sing   a   song. _____

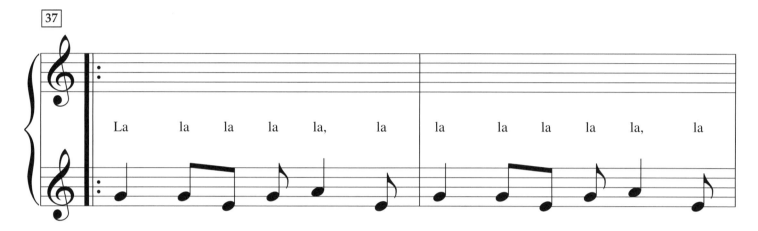

La   la   la   la   la,   la   la   la   la   la   la,   la

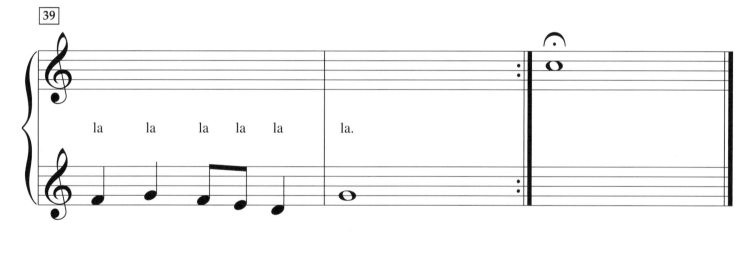

la   la   la   la   la   la.

The Syncopated Clock

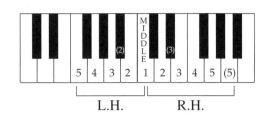

L.H.   R.H.

Music by Leroy Anderson
Words by Mitchell Parish

Moderately

mf

There was a man like you and me, ___ as
had a clock that worked all right. ___ It

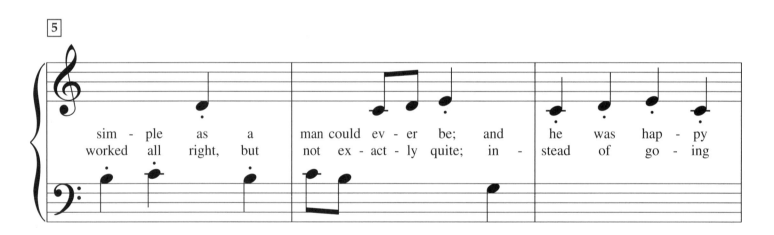

sim - ple as a man could ev - er be; and he was hap - py
worked all right, but not ex - act - ly quite; in - stead of go - ing

Duet Part (Student plays one octave higher than written.)

Moderately

mp

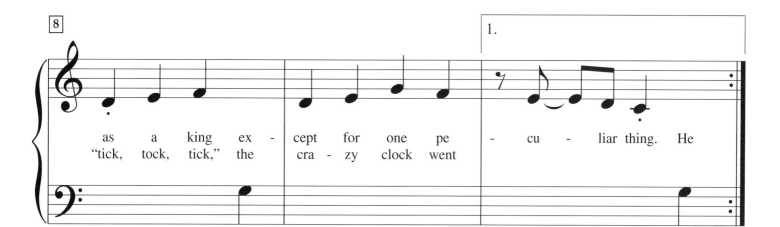

as a king ex - cept for one pe - cu - liar thing. He
"tick, tock, tick," the cra - zy clock went

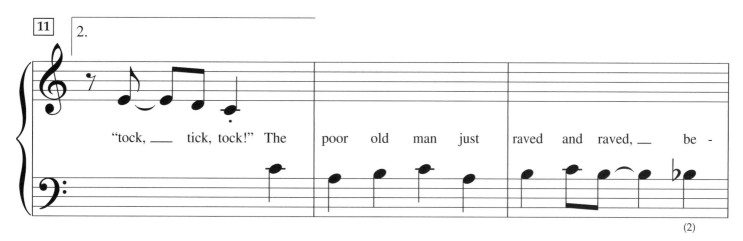

"tock, ___ tick, tock!" The poor old man just raved and raved, ___ be -

(2)

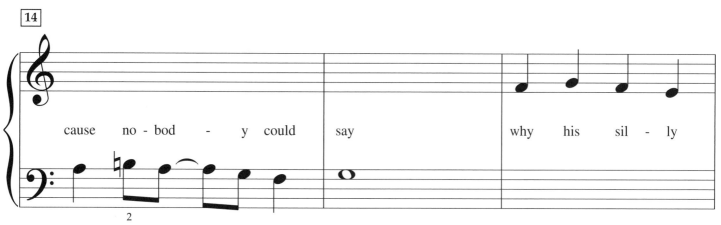

cause no - bod - y could say why his sil - ly

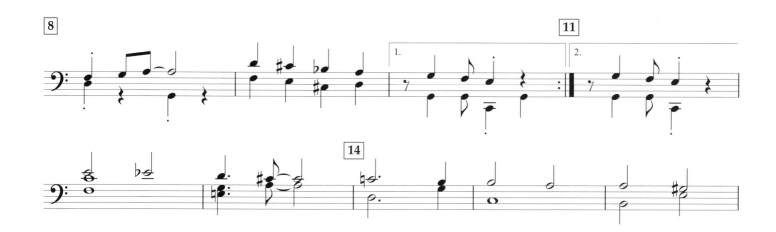

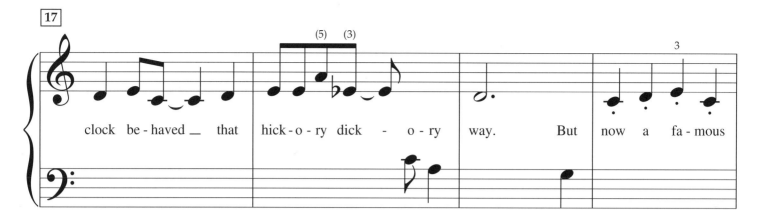

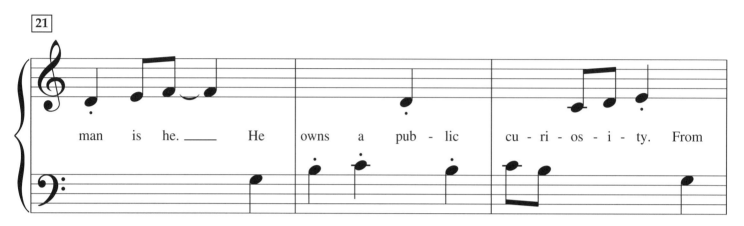

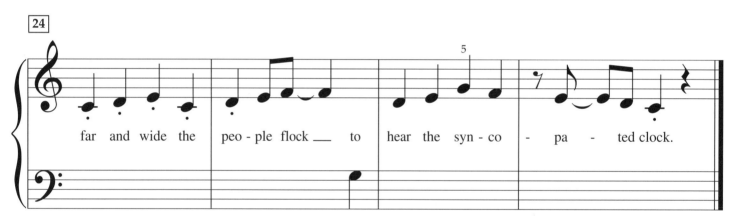

When I Grow Too Old to Dream

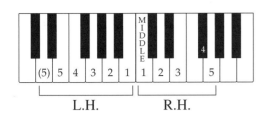

L.H.   R.H.

Lyrics by Oscar Hammerstein II
Music by Sigmund Romberg

Slowly

When I grow too old to dream,

I'll have you to re - mem - ber.

Duet Part (Student plays one octave higher than written.)

Slowly

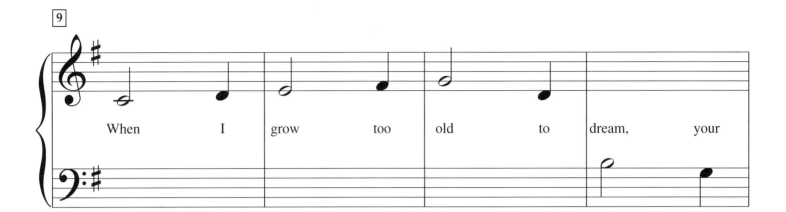

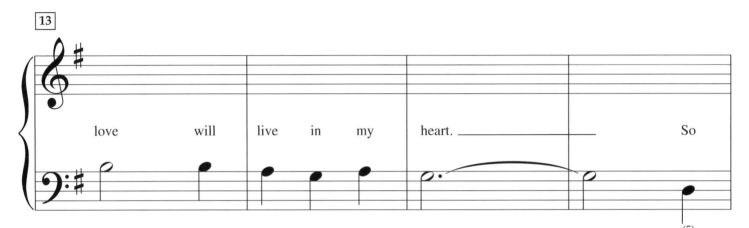

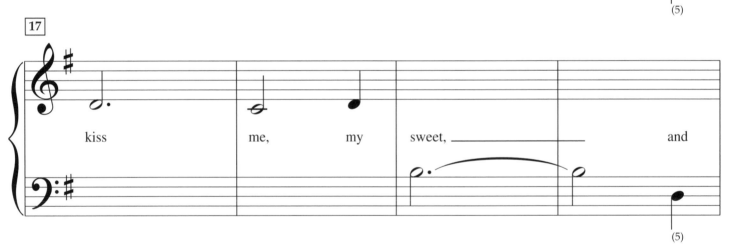

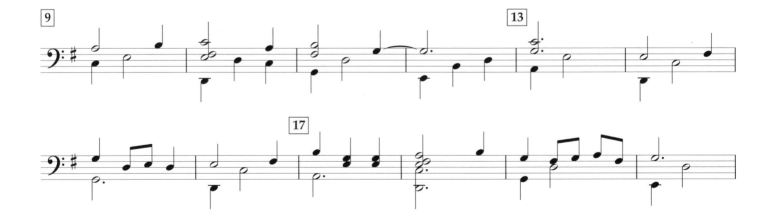

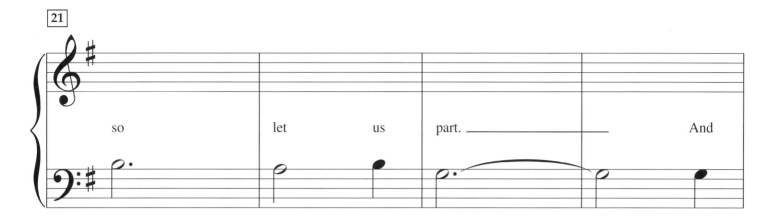

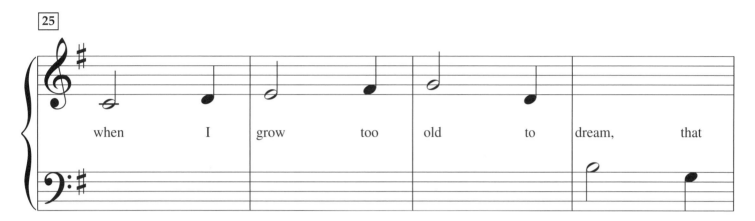

We're Off to See the Wizard

from THE WIZARD OF OZ

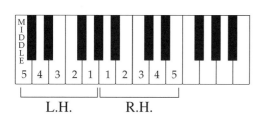

Lyric by E.Y. "Yip" Harburg
Music by Harold Arlen

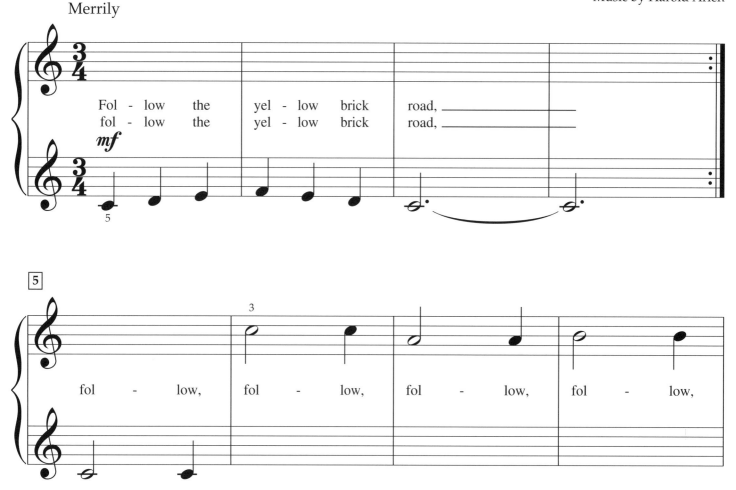

Merrily

Fol - low the yel - low brick road, ____
fol - low the yel - low brick road, ____

fol - low, fol - low, fol - low, fol - low,

Duet Part (Student plays as written.)

Merrily

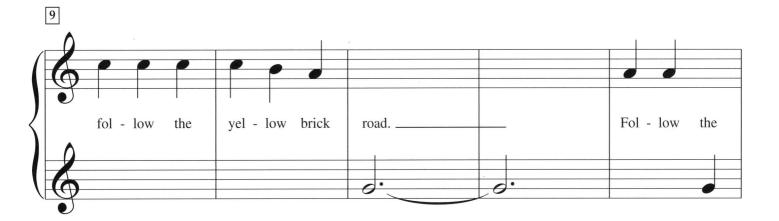

fol - low the   yel - low brick   road. _____   Fol - low   the

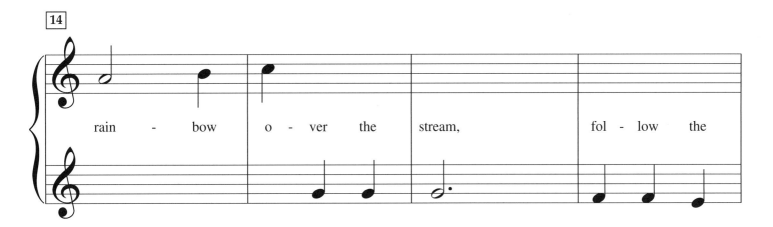

rain - bow   o - ver   the   stream,   fol - low   the

fel - low   who   fol - lows   a   dream,   fol - low,

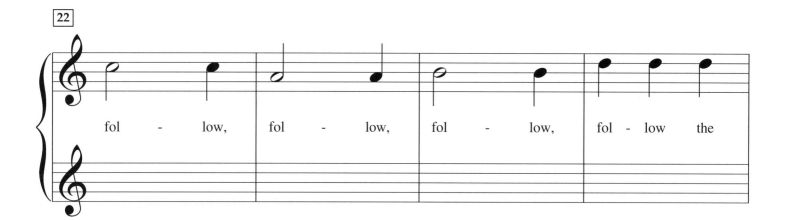

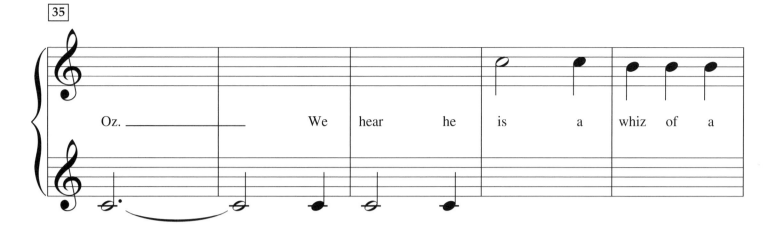

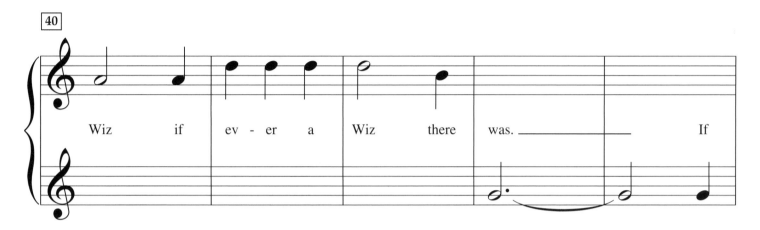

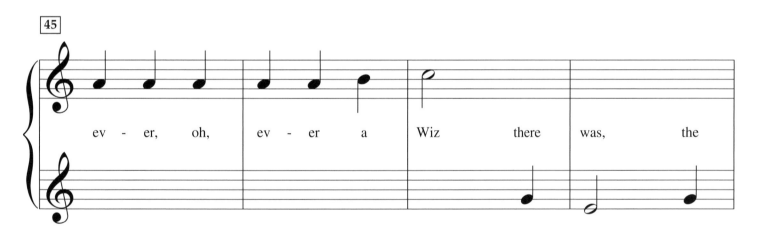

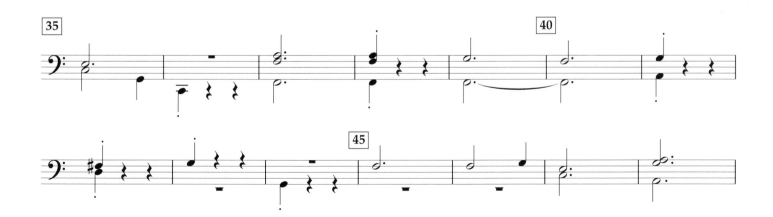

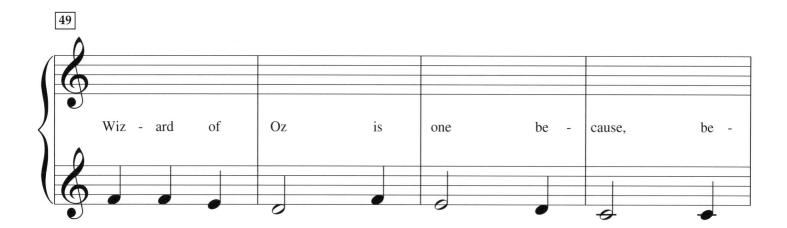

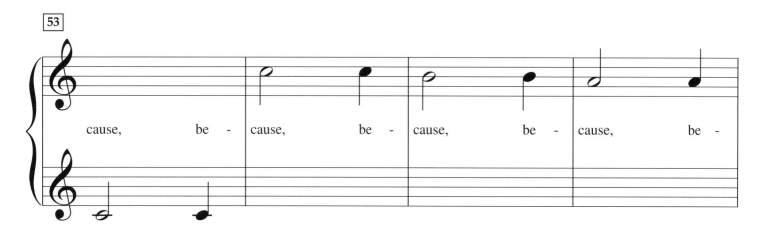

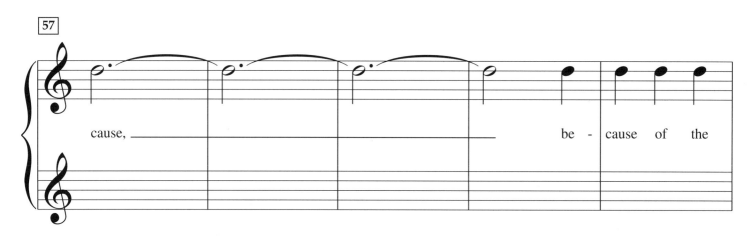

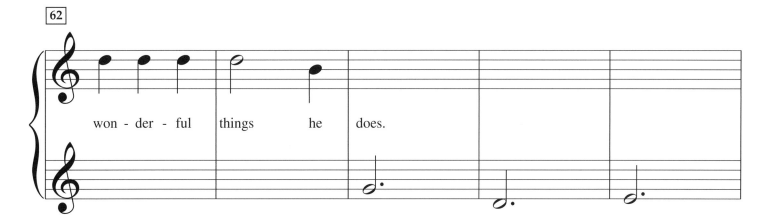

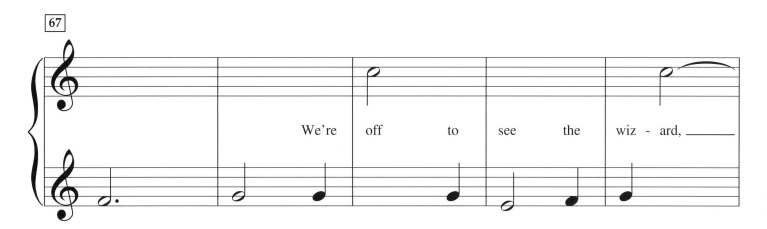

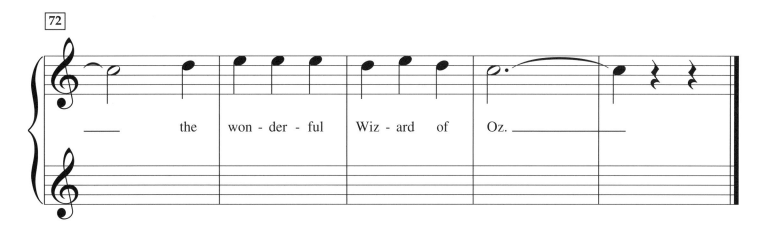

PLAYING PIANO HAS NEVER BEEN EASIER!

5-FINGER PIANO COLLECTIONS FROM HAL LEONARD

BEATLES! BEATLES!

8 classics, including: A Hard Day's Night • Hey Jude • Love Me Do • P.S. I Love You • Ticket to Ride • Twist and Shout • Yellow Submarine • Yesterday.
_____ 00292061 ....$8.99

CHILDREN'S TV FAVORITES

Themes from 8 Hit Shows

Five-finger arrangements of the themes for: Barney • Bob the Builder • Thomas the Tank Engine • Dragon Tales • PB&J Otter • SpongeBob SquarePants • Rugrats • Dora the Explorer.
_____ 00311208 ....$7.95

CHURCH SONGS FOR KIDS

Features five-finger arrangements of 15 sacred favorites, including: Amazing Grace • The B-I-B-L-E • Down in My Heart • Fairest Lord Jesus • Hallelu, Hallelujah! • I'm in the Lord's Army • Jesus Loves Me • Kum Ba Yah • My God Is So Great, So Strong and So Mighty • Oh, How I Love Jesus • Praise Him, All Ye Little Children • Zacchaeus and more.
_____ 00310613 .... $7.95

CLASSICAL FAVORITES – 2ND EDITION

arr. Carol Klose

Includes 12 beloved classical pieces from Bach, Bizet, Haydn, Grieg and other great composers: Bridal Chorus • Hallelujah! • He Shall Feed His Flock • Largo • Minuet in G • Morning • Rondeau • Surprise Symphony • To a Wild Rose • Toreador Song.
_____ 00310611 .... $7.95

CONTEMPORARY MOVIE HITS – 2ND EDITION

7 favorite songs from hit films: Go the Distance (Hercules) • My Heart Will Go On (Titanic) • When You Believe (The Prince of Egypt) • You'll Be in My Heart (Tarzan™) • You've Got a Friend in Me (Toy Story and Toy Story II) • more.
_____ 00310687 ....$7.95

DISNEY MOVIE FUN

8 classics, including: Beauty and the Beast • When You Wish Upon a Star • Whistle While You Work • and more.
_____ 00292067 .... $7.95

DISNEY TUNES

Includes: Can You Feel the Love Tonight? • Chim Chim Cher-ee • Go the Distance • It's a Small World • Supercalifragilisticexpialidocious • Under the Sea • You've Got a Friend in Me • Zero to Hero.
_____ 00310375 .... $7.95

SELECTIONS FROM DISNEY'S PRINCESS COLLECTION VOL. 1

7 songs sung by Disney heroines – with a full-color illustration of each! Includes: Colors of the Wind • A Dream Is a Wish Your Heart Makes • I Wonder • Just Around the Riverbend • Part of Your World • Something There • A Whole New World.
_____ 00310847 ....$7.95

EENSY WEENSY SPIDER & OTHER NURSERY RHYME FAVORITES

Includes 11 rhyming tunes kids love: Hickory Dickory Dock • Humpty Dumpty • Hush, Little Baby • Jack and Jill • Little Jack Horner • Mary Had a Little Lamb • Peter, Peter Pumpkin Eater • Pop Goes the Weasel • Tom, Tom, the Piper's Son • more.
_____ 00310465 .... $7.95

GOD BLESS AMERICA®

8 PATRIOTIC AND INSPIRATIONAL SONGS

Features 8 patriotic favorites anyone can play: America, the Beautiful • Battle Hymn of the Republic • God Bless America • My Country, 'Tis of Thee (America) • The Star Spangled Banner • This Is My Country • This Land Is Your Land • You're a Grand Old Flag.
_____ 00310828 ....$7.95

MOVIE MAGIC – 2ND EDITION

Seven gems from the silver screen arranged for beginners. Includes: Chariots of Fire • (Everything I Do) I Do It for You • Heart and Soul • I Will Always Love You • The Rainbow Connection • Summer Nights • Unchained Melody.
_____ 00310261 ....$7.95

THE SOUND OF MUSIC

8 big-note arrangements of popular songs from this perennial favorite musical, including: Climb Ev'ry Mountain • Do-Re-Mi • Edelweiss • The Lonely Goatherd • My Favorite Things • Sixteen Going on Seventeen • So Long, Farewell • The Sound of Music.
_____ 00310249 ....$8.99

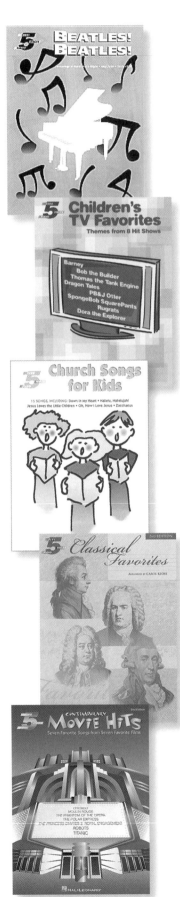

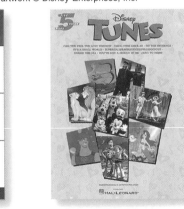

Prices, contents and availability subject to change without notice.

0612

Happy Birthday to You
and Other Great Songs

ISBN 978-1-4768-1291-5

HAL•LEONARD®
CORPORATION
7777 W. BLUEMOUND RD. P.O. BOX 13819 MILWAUKEE, WI 53213

Visit Hal Leonard Online at
www.halleonard.com